A Primer of

EZRA POUND

by M. L. Rosenthal

The Macmillan Company · New York · 1960

© M. L. Rosenthal 1960

First Printing

The Macmillan Company, New York
Brett-Macmillan Ltd., Galt, Ontario

Printed in the United States of America

Library of Congress catalog card number: 60-7281

Contents

1

The Early Poetry

Ezra Pound's career is so interlaced with the whole of modern letters and politics that one might devote many pages to it and never touch on his poetry. For a time at least this man of genuine learning and humanity put his great talents to the service of Mussolini and his Fascist party. Yet long before, even while being attracted to ideas which finally led him to this service, he had established himself as a prophet of the open spirit. "My province," he might have declared, "is all creative thought," for he began early to cultivate an eclecticism disciplined by rich understanding of a number of living traditions. His mind and sensibilities darted everywhere, and he encouraged many other writers of promise, whether Communist, Bohemian, proto-Nazi, or whatever, to do the best that was in them. His intelligence, indeed, has been a flowering of Western self-awareness, with life-bestowing and poisonous blossoms intermingled, as if all the beautiful vitality and all the brilliant rottenness of our heritage in its luxuriant variety were both at once made manifest in it.

Therefore, despite the considerable attention paid him by critics and scholars, relatively little has been said to distinguish Pound the poet from Pound the thinker, propagandist, and literary man of action. It is obvious, we must grant, that poet and man are in the long run inseparable. Nevertheless, the artist's reputation has suffered from the activist-thinker's vagaries and even from his achievements. In the *Cantos* especially, that great and complex enterprise of the last several decades, the two Pounds have interfered with each other. The interference, perhaps inevitable, has understandably confused all but the most devoted and professionally informed readers—and them also often enough. Hence their laudable concern to explain his unorthodox principles and his subtleties of method and allusion.

And yet this concern *can* be pushed too far. A normal reader who undertook, simply and innocently, to read *Personae: The Collected Poems* [1] from the beginning could go quite a distance without having to scream for the police or whistle for the experts. Here, among the poems written before Pound was twenty-five, one finds many direct, musical, lively pieces of fresh excellence still. The first of them, "The Tree," opens the book with a curious yet lucid imaginative projection, one incidentally which augurs the poet's later fascination with the motif of metamorphosis, so vital to the *Cantos*:

> I stood still and was a tree amid the wood,
> Knowing the truth of things unseen before;
> Of Daphne and the laurel bow
> And that god-feasting couple old
> That grew elm-oak amid the wold.

[1] New York: Horace Liveright, 1926; New Directions, 1949. All verse quotations, except from the *Cantos,* are from the 1949 edition.

The early poems, too, give frank evidence of his study of the Provençal troubadours, and of Browning and his vigorous, idiomatic roughnesses as well. Thus, "Na Audiart" begins as pure song and word-play:

> Though thou well dost wish me ill
> Audiart, Audiart . . .

But later in the same poem, we hear the unmistakable ring of old R. B.:

> Just a word in thy praise, girl,
> Just for the swirl
> Thy satins make upon the stair . . . .

Even these brief snatches, with their melodic variations of line-length, their skillful play on certain vowels and consonants, their certainty of phrasing, will show how precocious a student of his masters Pound was. At this point he was still in the grip of the late-Romantic tradition as it had come to him by way of the British nineties. The themes are all familiar: the sentimental egocentrism of the artist in "Famam Librosque Cano"; the yearning for spiritual freedom and the company of kindred sensibilities of "In Durance" ("But I am homesick after mine own kind"); the mingled pathos, romance, and comedy of "Marvoil." Even when he is most derivative and imitative, however, Pound's style is charged with a certain essential, idiosyncratic energy. Witness the boisterously insulting epithets of "Marvoil":

> All for one half-bald, knock-knee'd king of the Aragonese,
> Alfonso, Quattro, poke-nose.

The best known of the earlier pieces, probably, are "Sestina: Altaforte" and "Ballad of the Goodly Fere." In "Altaforte," a work of pure exuberant bombast in a tricky Provençal pattern, Bertrans de Born raves gorgeously of war's delights and the swinishness of peace-lovers. "For the death of such sluts I go rejoicing," he shouts, and Pound's introduction to the poem has equal gusto: "Dante Alighieri put this man in hell for that he was a stirrer up of strife. Eccovi! Judge ye! Have I dug him up again?" The poem is a brilliant, intentionally one-dimensional composition, studded with clanging monosyllables that hammer out the obsession of a blood-drunk brute. Bertrans' outcries are spectacularly spondaic and alliterative. "Damn it all!" he bellows; "all this our South stinks peace." His black piety is uncompromising: "May God damn for ever all who cry 'Peace!'" He "prays" indiscriminately to Heaven and to Hell, and with onomatopoeic fervor: "Hell grant soon we hear again the swords clash!" Pound is said to have roared out the "Sestina" in a Soho restaurant when it was first written, shocking the genteel bourgeois patrons of the place. Its self-evident technical virtuosity, praised highly by T. S. Eliot among others, thus contributed incidentally and in a small way to the disconcertment of British philistinism: one of the poet's minor aims at least.

The much-anthologized, virile-posturing "Ballad of the Goodly Fere" presents Jesus as "No capon priest" but a "man o' men" especially fond of other "brawny men" and of "ships and the open sea," a scornfully laughing Nietzschean Robin Hood (with dashes of Whitman and Kipling) who drives out the money-changers "Wi' a bundle o' cords swung free." He resembles the risen Dionysus rather more than the gentle Christ. Alien to gentility, he is of the implacable, pre-Classical host of divinities:

> I ha' seen him eat o' the honey-comb
> Sin' they nailed him to the tree.

Though forced and overextended, the ballad illustrates Pound's extraordinary ease with traditional forms and his never-ending search for ways to bring these forms, and traditional themes as well, into renewed if unexpected life.

He turns them to his own use, making a triumph of what might otherwise be a mere exercise and creating, as the critic Ronald Duncan has said of "Altaforte," "a boisterous vitality within the confines of the form." [2]

Pound gives his game away more vulnerably in "The Flame," which reveals the depth and implications of his commitment to medieval Provençal values as he found them in Arnaut Daniel and others. [3] In the greatness of Provence he found a reinforcement of the revived Romantic idealism he shared with Yeats and Joyce, among many other writers. Indeed, "The Flame" begins as though composed by Yeats, Joyce, and Pound in committee:

> 'Tis not a game that plays at mates and mating,
> Provence knew;
> 'Tis not a game of barter, lands, and houses,
> Provence knew;
> We who are wise beyond your dream of wisdom,
> Drink our immortal moments; we "pass through."
> We have gone forth beyond your bonds and borders,
> Provence knew;
> And all the tales of Oisin say but this:
> That man doth pass the net of days and hours. . . .

While each of these three writers has a strain of unrelenting materialism in his make-up, each has also this softer idealism in his work, especially in his earlier writings. All have shown enormous faith in the symbol-making power of art as a gift enabling us to "pass through" toward the ineffable. If eventually theirs is a secular way of thought, it remains a secular *religiosity* which substitutes aesthetic creativity for godhead. "Provence knew" that there is more to love than its sensual and its socially practical aspects; the added dimension, the "more," was the creation of the poetic

---

[2] "Poet's Poet," in *Ezra Pound*, ed. Peter Russell (London: Peter Nevill Ltd., 1950), p. 160.
[3] See Ezra Pound, *Literary Essays* (Norfolk, Conn.: New Directions, 1954), pp. 91–200.

imagination. It was the troubadours who had made religious vision of the profane, blasphemous rituals of the Court of Love:

> Search not my lips, O Love, let go my hands,
> This thing that moves as man is no more mortal.

Certain passages in "The Flame" glow beyond the rest of this uneven poem, with its sentimental spiritualities in awkward places. (The passage just quoted is one illustration of such bogging-down.) On the whole, though, it remains a program-poem—that is, one written primarily to clarify the writer's perspectives to himself. Pound's craftsmanship comes off better in the graceful "Ballatetta": a vision of the Beloved in the best troubadour tradition, and without the overreaching preachments of "The Flame." First we see her as a living being, surrounded by an aureole that "doth melt us into song." And thereupon the song itself takes over the poem:

> The broken sunlight for a healm she beareth
> Who hath my heart in jurisdiction. . . .

"Ballatetta" gives us one of the earliest of the shining moments of exultant vision, suffused with imagery of light, in Pound's poetry. Its success in adapting formal achievements outside the English tradition to the needs of our language is directly related to his never-ending involvement with problems of translation and his boldness in dealing with them.

Perhaps, though, we should not speak of Provençal or any other European poetry as "outside the English tradition." To Pound as to Eliot "the tradition" is something antedating and transcending any one national or linguistic segment of it. At one time, after all, he had been a student of great promise in the Romance languages, a graduate fellow and instructor at the University of Pennsylvania. His purpose in first going abroad in 1906 had been to gather materials for a doctoral dissertation on Lope de Vega. It was natural for him, as natural as for any person of effective education, to think of tradition not as narrow conventionalism but as a driving force in the modern spirit: "a beauty which we preserve and not a set of fetters to bind us," he wrote in 1913.[4] But it took rare understanding to see just how this force can leap across the barriers of language and in what sense, exactly, the melic poets of seventh and sixth century Greece (B.C.) and the Provençal poets might be considered the founders of the two great lyric traditions of the West. "From the first arose practically all the poetry of the 'ancient world,' from the second practically all that of the modern." [5] In both these great sources "the arts of music and verse were most closely knit together" and "each thing done by the poet had some definite musical urge or necessity bound up within it."

Thus, Pound's interest in such poets as Sappho, Arnaut Daniel, Cavalcanti, and Dante (the full list goes beyond Greek and Provençal poetry; an entire curriculum of reading is outlined in *The ABC of Reading* and elsewhere) grows out of a need for models of organic composition. That is, he sought poetry in which sound, sense, and image must be functions of one another. Like Picasso with his thorough classical grounding, Pound has made his knowledge of tradition count toward the originality of his own artistry. One of the great experimentalists of our century is thus, almost inevitably, in another sense the foremost traditionalist of our day. Pound's essay on Cavalcanti (which he developed and modified from 1910 to 1931, maintaining a constant goal while his writing was undergoing its most important changes) defines the kind of poetic vision he has always been after:

We appear to have lost the radiant world where one thought cuts through another with clean edge, a world of moving energies . . . , magnetisms that take form, that are seen, or that border the visible, the matter of Dante's *paradiso*, the

---

[4] *Ibid.*, p. 91.
[5] *Ibid.*

glass under water, the form that seems a form seen in a mirror. . . . Not the pagan worship of strength, nor the Greek perception of visual non-animate plastic, or plastic in which the being animate was not the main and principal quality, but this 'harmony in the sentience' or harmony of the sentient, . . . where stupid men have not reduced all 'energy' to unbounded undistinguished abstraction.

For the modern scientist energy has no borders, it is a shapeless 'mass' of force; even his capacity to differentiate it to a degree never dreamed by the ancients has not led him to think of its shape or even its loci. The rose that his magnet makes in the iron filings, does not lead him to think of the force in botanic terms, or wish to visualize that force as floral and extant. . . .

A medieval 'natural philosopher' would find this modern world full of enchantments, not only the light in the electric bulb, but the thought of the current hidden in air and in wire would give him a mind full of forms. . . . The medieval philosopher would probably have been unable to think the electric world, and *not* think of it as a world of forms. . . . Or possibly this will fall under the eye of a contemporary scientist of genius who will answer: But, damn you, that is exactly what we do feel; or under the eye of a painter who will answer: Confound you, you *ought* to find just that in my painting.[6]

Now all these ideas about past and present, about science and Provence and the neglected universe of forms, converge for Pound in certain crucial attitudes toward craftsmanship. The poet's created world is, ideally, that of Dante: a "radiant" world in which "one thought cuts through another with clean edge, a world of moving energies." Whatever the feelings and ideas he expresses, they must be embodied in a form precise in outline but crackling with the living conception which has given them birth. As these attitudes develop, Pound begins to lay enormous emphasis on the single image, insisting that properly understood it "is an intellectual and emotional complex in an instant of time" and becoming the dynamic instigator of the Imagist movement.

[6] *Ibid.*, pp. 154–155.

The classic example of Imagism is generally held to be H. D.'s "Oread," but Pound's own "In a Station of the Metro" is a richer, more compressed example:

> The apparition of these faces in the crowd;
> Petals on a wet, black bough.

The effect of this pure, direct image of fragile, destroyed beauty against its dark background—the aftermath of a rainstorm, perhaps—is compounded of a fusion of numerous nearly invisible "hints": first, a combined affection, helpless "appreciation," and dismay at all these glimpses of faces ("apparitions") in their subway-world of semidarkness; at the same time, a related, elusive suggestion of shades of the damned in Avernus; and along with these impressions, an implied criticism of modern civilization.

Here in miniature is the visualization of "force in botanic terms," the provision of "borders" to define the "shape" and "loci" of contemporary experience. Another example, completely removed this time from a particular urban setting yet bearing much the same meaning, is the poem "April":

> Three spirits came to me
> And drew me apart
> To where the olive boughs
> Lay stripped upon the ground:
> Pale carnage beneath bright mist.

As in the "Metro" poem, the final line brings the whole to a sharp point of pregnant concentration. (In both poems, incidentally, Pound uses the consonants *p* and *b* to help prepare us for, and then to plunge us into, this intensification at the end.) The "stripped" boughs beneath the blossom-laden tree arouse the same kind of compassion that the blown petals stuck on the slick black bough do in "Metro." The "spirits" resemble the faces in the "apparition" there, and the "bright mist" of flowers suggests something infinitely delicate and desirable, now lost forever. Contemplating both poems,

we will perhaps recall Homer's description of the multi-
tudinous dead in the *Odyssey*, an abbreviated translation of
which Pound was to provide in the first of the *Cantos*:

> Souls out of Erebus, cadaverous dead, of brides
> Of youths and of the old who had borne much;
> Souls stained with recent tears, girls tender . . .[7]

In "April" itself Pound underlines the tragic juxtaposition of
"pale carnage" with bright loveliness by his Latin epigraph:
"*Nympharum membra disjecta*" (scattered limbs of the
nymphs).

"April" and "In a Station of the Metro" are from the
volume *Lustra,* containing poems written between 1912 and
1915. Pound's mastery, by his late twenties, of poetic line
and metaphor is well illustrated by the two poems just ex-
amined. In the volume as a whole, he tries many modes of
writing—Catullan satire, light impressionist pieces, rhetorical
forays (including an address to Walt Whitman as his "pig-
headed father" with whom he is now ready to make a "pact"),
witticisms and manifestoes of various sorts. Here is the
arresting "Coitus," its startling initial figure one instance
among many of the sexual and phallic motifs central to
much of Pound's most serious work:

> The gilded phaloi of the crocuses
>   are thrusting at the spring air.

Here is "The Coming of War: Actaeon," with its restless,
ominous movement:

> A sea
> Harsher than granite,
>   unstill, never ceasing . . .

And here is the perfect classicism of "The Spring," intro-

[7] *The Cantos of Ezra Pound* (New York: New Directions, 1948),
p. 3. All quotations from *Cantos* 1–84 are from this edition.

ducing its nostalgic theme of lost love with a Sapphic sure-
ness:

> Cydonian Spring with her attendant train,
> Maelids and water-girls,
> Stepping beneath a boisterous wind from Thrace . . .

After this start the poem speeds through its description of
how Spring "spreads the bright tips" of newness everywhere.
Then suddenly the personification is dropped in a rush of
bitter memory:

> And wild desire
> Falls like black lightning.
> O bewildered heart,
> Though every branch have back what last year lost,
> She, who moved here amid the cyclamen,
> Moves only now a clinging tenuous ghost.

The difference between a poem like this one and a poem
like "The Flame" does not lie in any absence of *feeling* in
the former. But the feeling of "The Spring" is rooted in the
poem's physical, sensuous imagery rather than in abstract
Romanticism. A few years later, in 1917, Pound was to pro-
claim, a little stridently, that the genuine poetry of this century would "move against poppycock":

it will be harder and saner, it will be . . . 'nearer the bone.'
It will be as much like granite as it can be, its force will lie
in its truth, its interpretative power (of course, poetic force
does always rest there). . . . We will have fewer painted
adjectives impending the shock and stroke of it. At least for
myself, I want it so, austere, direct, free from emotional
slither.[8]

It was this rejection of "emotional slither" that led to
Pound's parody of Housman:

[8] *Literary Essays*, p. 12.

O woe, woe,
People are born and die,
We also shall be dead pretty soon
Therefore let us act as if we were
dead already.

It helps account, too, for the appeal to him of Heine, like
Pound a rebel armoring his sensitivity in the ironic mail of
a lively intelligence. Thus, Pound's translation from Die
Heimkehr:

The mutilated choir boys
When I begin to sing
Complain about the awful noise
And call my voice too thick a thing.

And it throws light on Pound's ambivalent feelings toward
Whitman. If it be true that many sons spend their lives
revising, in their own behavior, the images of their fathers,
we may say, allowing ourselves the license of Pound's own
simile in "A Pact," that he took over Walt's vision of the
poet-prophet and poet-teacher and recast it in a more sophis-
ticated and Europeanized, a more formally demanding mold.
Yet, though we can glance at the question only in passing
here, there remains a closer kinship between these two than
at first would appear likely. The largeness of their concerns,
the sprawling epic character of their major efforts, their
attempts to encompass a multitude of contradictory elements
through main force, and the revolutionary quality of their
careers lock them into undeniable kinship.

Still, Pound's interest in "hardness," in "the tradition,"
and in the poetry of pure vision do conceal this kinship very
efficiently. His growth toward realization of this combined
interest had been perfectly evident even before *Lustra*, certainly at least as early as the 1912 *Ripostes*. By this time he
had undergone an arduous apprenticeship in translation, and
it now bore fruit in one of his best known successes, the
rendering of the Anglo-Saxon "The Seafarer" into modern

English. Though it contains more Wardour Street English than it should, the poem is vastly successful in its opening section, and in isolated later portions. The success is due in part to Pound's marvelous ear, in part to the fact that Old English metric and alliteration are unusually congenial to his special talents. The Anglo-Saxon *kenning* may be seen as a frozen Imagist metaphor, and the plaintive melancholy of the monologue, crammed with detail but held to a single emotional pitch, is not far removed from the characteristic modern lyric-contemplative poem. The failure of the translation to sustain interest at every point is not altogether Pound's fault; the original was always, in our temerarious view, too long for its own good. In *Ripostes* also we find the mysterious "Portrait d'une Femme," a compassionate yet satirical characterization which is at the same time a remarkable example of what skillful accenting and the bravura manipulation of a few sounds (especially the pivotal *yū*-sound here) can accomplish. "The Return," one of Pound's most beautiful and economical poems, is a triumph of accentual variation in its wavering opening notes, its gathering of full-blooded speed and strength, and then its hesitant falling-off again. Finally, "The Alchemist," a "chant for the transmutation of metals," is one of our great incantatory poems. As in "The Return," where the hero-gods of the past are through an effort of poetic conjuring brought up into the foreground of consciousness, the vision emerges with the strange clarity of aesthetic transformation fully realized:

> As you move among the bright trees;
> As your voices, under the larches of Paradise
> Make a clear sound . . . .

The Pound we have been reviewing is the ardent and committed young poet who believed in the life of art as few men have ever believed in it. He is the man of whom Carl Sandburg could once say that he was "the best man writing poetry today" while T. S. Eliot, whose direction was so thoroughly different from Sandburg's, could echo Dante's praise of Arnaut Daniel by calling Pound *"il miglior fabbro,"* the finest craftsman. Of Pound's poem "The Return" Yeats wrote that "it gives me better words than my own." The work of the later Pound, author of *Hugh Selwyn Mauberley* and the *Cantos,* is solidly based on what he had done by 1915, when he became thirty years old.

2

Basic Frames of Thought

Ezra Pound's commitment to his art is the rationale of that art. Out of it comes the impulse to the longer works, in large degree, and to his larger theoretical interests. It is the key to his fundamental belief in the importance of literature to the state:

Has literature a function in the state . . . ? It has. . . . It has to do with the clarity and vigour of 'any and every' thought and opinion. It has to do with maintaining the very cleanliness of the tools, the health of the very matter of thought itself. . . . The individual cannot think and communicate his thought, the governor and legislator cannot act effectively or frame his laws, without words, and the solidity and validity of these words is in the care of the damned and despised *litterati*. When their work goes rotten—by that I do not mean when they express indecorous thoughts—but when their very medium, the very essence of their work, the application of word to thing goes rotten, i.e. becomes slushy and inexact, or excessive or bloated, the whole machinery of social and of individual thought and order goes to pot. This is a lesson of history. . . .[9]

Now whether Pound was right in saying that the health of individual and state depends on the soundness of the language, which it is the writer's sacred task to maintain, or whether perhaps the relationship is just the reverse, or whether, finally, both literature and the state depend on unfathomable, or only partly fathomable, sources we need not try to determine here and now. Whatever the ultimate truth of the matter, there should certainly be general assent to the proposition that the status and integrity of letters is vitally related to the condition of society. Simply to begin thinking about this relationship is to raise the poet out of the musical-doll category to which he is usually relegated.

Pound has always been sharply conscious of the way in which poetry bespeaks the values of whole peoples, bringing to the surface not only their more cheerful wisdom but also their deeply, often secretly and inarticulately felt unorthodoxies of real sentiment. Moreover, he believes literally that the loyalty of genuine poets to sound workmanship and to the meanings of tradition is a kind of guardianship of principled standards in the republic at large, whether in general communication, in the economic life, or in the functioning of government.

We must bear these attitudes in mind most especially when we come to *Mauberley* and the *Cantos*. The first portion of the *Mauberley* sequence is in large part a denunciation of our society's denial to the dedicated poet of his rightful place. Academic and editorial stuffiness and venality, it argues, shoddiness in every phase of human activity, and that final criminal betrayal, the World War, have made for a "botched civilization." At the war's end, the poet-speaker sizes up what is left of this civilization, noting above all the

[9] *Ibid.*, p. 21.

triumph of insensitivity and mass-production tinniness over responsibility and true craftsmanship. The bureaucratic expropriation of literature by businesslike "operators" is, he sees, marked also, and quite logically, by the serious poet's loss of most means of livelihood, literary patronage having in any case passed out of the picture some while back. The speaker considers retreat or self-exile, but summons up his own courage for the time being at least. Against "liars in public places" and the triumphs of "usury age-old" he sets the memory of "Young blood and high blood" sacrificed in the War:

> Charm, smiling at the good mouth,
> Quick eyes gone under earth's lid . . . .

Against the new type of professional who gives him practical tips on the literary game—

> And give up verse, my boy,
> There's nothing in it—

he sets the poets of the nineties, Yeats's friends Dowson and Johnson, who stuck by their poetic guns at all costs (and the costs *were* cruel), and the whole great literary tradition from Homer and Bion through Villon, Shakespeare, and Waller to such moderns as Flaubert, Gautier, and Henry James.[10] His own role he defines as that of a contemporary Odysseus who has either mistaken his heroic mission or undertaken it in the wrong century:

> For three years, out of key with his time,
> He strove to resuscitate the dead art
> Of poetry; to maintain "the sublime"
> In the old sense. . . .

[10] John Espey, *Ezra Pound's* Mauberley (Berkeley and Los Angeles: University of California Press, 1955), traces the literary ancestry informing *Mauberley* painstakingly and convincingly. This volume also contains a superior text of the sequence, although our quotations are taken from *Personae* for the reader's convenience.

But we shall have a fuller look at *Mauberley* and its ironies shortly. If we turn now to the *Cantos,* Pound's chief work-in-progress for a great many years, we find the function of literature and the other arts in the state a central point of focus in it again and again, a critical element in the entire problem of cultural stability. Canto 13 shows Kung (Confucius) saying to his disciples:

. . . "When the prince has gathered about him
"All the savants and artists, his riches will be fully employed."

A corollary of this principle is Kung's warning to the lute-player Tian:

. . . "Without character you will
            be unable to play on that instrument
Or to execute the music fit for the Odes. . . ."

In shocking, purposeful contrast to the ordered Confucian reasonableness of such pronouncements, the next canto, with Swiftian violence, explodes a nightmare picture of our modern inferno of corruption and profiteering, dominion of that deadliest evil, Usury. Integral to the scene are the howling, stinking "betrayers of language," those "perverts, who have set money-lust before the pleasure of the senses":

The slough of unamiable liars,
        bog of stupidities,
malevolent stupidities, and stupidities,
the soil living pus, full of vermin,
dead maggots begetting live maggots,
        slum owners,
usurers squeezing crab-lice, pandars to authority,
pets-de-loup, sitting on piles of stone books,
obscuring the texts with philology,
        hiding them under their persons,
the air without refuge of silence,
        the drift of lice, teething . . . .

Here is the very opposite of the voices heard "under the larches of Paradise" in "The Alchemist" and also, again, elsewhere in the *Cantos*. Subtle in detail, the rhythm is obvious enough in its general pattern, which has two basic characteristics. First, there is a line of rising force, often mounting to a hovering accent (a succession of two or more stressed syllables giving the effect of unremitting emphasis) toward the middle and then shifting to a falling rhythm at the very end (líars, vérmin, and so on). Second, there is a series, with exceptions and variations, of alternating longer and shorter phrases. Alliteration and the repetition of key words, a profusion of spitting sibilants and stop-sounds, and the echoing of vowels and of the dyings-off of line-endings support this pattern. Together these effects create an atmosphere of absolute revulsion and contempt for the "usurers" and their hangers-on.

"Usury" is the black particular enemy in this war-chant of hate, as it is throughout the *Cantos*. In an essay which sums up Pound's economic theories fairly clearly and altogether sympathetically, Max Wykes-Joyce writes:

. . . it is a fact that our banking systems are based on usury, no matter by what sweeter name we call it to salve our troubled consciences, or to shrive ourselves of some atavistic condemnation. Hence Pound's first modification of the commonly held view of the function of banks. The levying of interest whether at two per cent. or twenty per cent. is usurious, and usury stands condemned as strongly in this American's view as it did in the teaching of the medieval Fathers.

In all his economic writings, he makes the basic distinction between banks founded for the good of their shareholders and regardless of the wellbeing of any and everyone else, which means almost all banks as we now know them; and banks founded primarily for the good of the whole people. . . .[11]

To illustrate, Wykes-Joyce calls our attention to Canto 71,

[11] Max Wykes-Joyce, "Some Considerations Arising from Ezra Pound's Conception of the Bank," in *Ezra Pound*, p. 218.

in which John Adams is quoted in a passage Pound himself
marks by a bold vertical line along the margin:

> Every bank of discount is downright corruption
> taxing the public for private individuals' gain.
> and if I say this in my will
> the American people wd/ pronounce I died crazy.

Pound's thinking on economics is thus not without very
respectable antecedents. Though strongly influenced by
C. H. Douglas, it is like all his thinking even more strongly
individual than derivative. In a sense, the viewpoint is an
aesthetic one: If economic relationships are bound within
limiting, non-organic forms, change the forms. "Make it
new!" The conception is primarily of a functional adaptation
of currency and credit procedures to the realities of a people's
needs and potential productivity in such a way that irre-
sponsible, destructive money-speculation becomes impossible.
The program is certainly attractive, but obviously it presents
very great difficulties and allows room for as much cynical
jargonizing and rhetorical manipulation as the market will
bear—and more. Hence its attractiveness to the theorists and
apologists of the Fascist state. But though it would take an
expert economist *and* student of semantics to pursue this
question to its ultimate implications beyond all the crack-
potism, double talk, and vaguenesses, clearly it does open up
certain real possibilities of social reform and justice and
derives from an idealistic and honorable tradition.

It is impossible to say that Pound's record in these matters
is without stain. His specific commitments to Mussolini's
methods and his anti-Semitism (see Canto 52, for instance),
which not even admirers as intelligent and well informed as
Wykes-Joyce, Hugh Kenner, and Brian Soper can very convincingly discount or explain away, remain the terrible
aberrations of a man of genius. Yet in the face of these im-
ponderables and of his own insufferable dogmatism, we are
compelled to recognize, in his poetry at its best, the humane
motives and the moral and intellectual power of his essential

outlook. It is then, we feel, that he is a child of the Enlightenment after all, of Voltaire and the Encyclopaedists, and that his satires and harangues are quite something else than special pleading for a vicious system of thought and behavior. There is in them the hard ironic honesty and anger against chicanery of Swift's "A Modest Proposal" or, in their less ferocious moments, of Thomas Love Peacock's *Crotchet Castle,* in which we read: "I have always understood . . . that promises to pay ought not to be kept; the essence of a safe and economical currency being an interminable series of broken promises." (See, in this connection, the closing section of Canto 88.)

Moreover, we must remember that Pound's fundamental criticism of modern society has the profound assent, admittedly with every conceivable variation of ideological shading, of almost the whole contemporary artistic community. An instance is the comment of his old friend William Carlos Williams, generally aware as he was of Pound's shortcomings, on a conversation with him during a visit in St. Elizabeth's Hospital (Washington, D.C.). Pound was confined there as a paranoiac after World War II until 1958, and it was only because of this commitment that he was not tried for treason because of his wartime propaganda broadcasts from Italy to American troops. Williams writes:

Do we have to be idiots dreaming in the semi-obscurities of a twilight mood to be poets? The culmination of our human achievement, all that we desire, can't be achieved by closing our eyes to a veritable wall barring our path. The theme of the poem must at such a point be the removal of the block to everything we might achieve once that barrier is removed. If we are to be taxed out of existence to feed private loans, the revenue from which is used by an international gang to perpetuate armed conflicts, at private profit—to further enrich the same gang—that, the inferno of the *Cantos,* must be one of the poet's nearest concerns.

So we talked, of who is in the know, as against the self-interested mob of "legislators," the pitiful but grossly ignorant big-shots who play in with the criminals—in city, state and nations; of our first duty as artists, the only semi-informed men of the community, whose sweep is the whole field of knowledge. It is our duty at all costs to speak; at all costs, even imprisonment in such isolation, such quarantine, from the spread of information as a St. Elizabeth's affords.[12]

"Usury," to return now to our consideration of Pound's leading ideas, is in Pound's thought *the* sin around which all others cluster. Sometimes he prefers the Latin form *Usura,* because of its medieval connotations. "With *Usura,*" Canto 45 tells us,

> no picture is made to endure nor to live with
> but it is made to sell and sell quickly
> with usura, sin against nature,
> is thy bread ever more of stale rags
> is thy bread dry as paper,
> with no mountain wheat, no strong flour
> with usura the line grows thick
> with usura is no clear demarcation . . . .

The incantatory, rhetorical, insistent beat of the argument and the parallelisms rises and rises in intensity until, by another path but with equal overbearing concentration of passion, it comes at the very end to a climax like that of Blake's "London." The similarity to Blake is in fact so striking as to throw a blazing light upon Pound's Canto 16 also, as we shall soon see. Blake's catalogue of the evils rotting away the city of London because of the triumph of property exploitation ("chartering") over love and fraternity culminates in one final staggering accusation:

> But most thro' midnight streets I hear
> How the youthful Harlot's curse
> Blasts the new born Infant's tear,
> And blights with plagues the Marriage hearse.

[12] *The Autobiography of William Carlos Williams* (New York: Random House, 1951), pp. 337–338.

And Pound's Canto 45 concludes:

> Usura slayeth the child in the womb
> It stayeth the young man's courting
> It hath brought palsey to bed, lyeth
> between the young bride and her bridegroom
>   CONTRA NATURAM
> They have brought whores for Eleusis
> Corpses are set to banquet
> at behest of usura.

That is to say: The sacred mysteries of love and sex, the cycles of nature, and the rituals of pagan tradition derived from these mysteries and cycles, all inherited in altered form by us together with the most hallowed taboos preserving the untouchableness of human privacy, are now violated in the name of money-power. Such is the final effect of the destruction of meaning and communication. Pound uses all his great skill successfully here in bringing together his feeling for these neglected sources of value and his location of their betrayal in a false principle of social order.

Against the hell of the usurers' dominions the poet repeatedly opposes his vision of the Earthly Paradise. It is a composite vision, drawn from Biblical, Grecian, Provençal, and Dantean imagery and from a wide acquaintance with mythologies and literatures. But its outstanding features are purity and clarity of color and light, together with the classically calm dignity of the figures that move upon its eternally luminous landscape:

> Then light air, under saplings,
> the blue banded lake under æther,
>   an oasis, the stones, the calm field . . . .
>   (Canto 16)

> Grove hath its altar
>   under elms, in that temple, in silence
> a lone nymph by the pool.
>   (Canto 90)

The light now, not of the sun.
　　　　　　Chrysophrase,
And the water green clear, and blue clear . . . .

Zagreus, feeding his panthers,
　　　　　　the turf clear as on hills under light.
And under the almond-trees, gods,
　　　　　　with them, *choros nympharum*. Gods . . . .
　　　　　　　　　　　　　　(Canto 17)

The dream of repose and quiet projected in this enchanted
light no doubt reflects a deeply psychological need on the
poet's part. But it is much more than his private "escape"
through self-indulgent revery. Pound's visions are conceived
as completely serious and relevant to life's most pressing
meanings; they even have "scientific" validity in the sense
advanced in his Cavalcanti essay, the sense of the "radiant"
and significant "world of forms" or of "moving energies"
which creates those meanings. The secular and aesthetic
religiosity they express is built around the "life-force," to use
a term now somewhat hackneyed but still much to the point.
At the heart of all the values, therefore, which "Usura" seeks
to slay is that same life-force. Its patron-divinity is Zagreus
(Dionysus, Bacchus), seen "feeding his panthers" in the
passage just quoted from Canto 17. Son of Zeus and Ceres,
he is the god of fertility and of allied mysteries, and is
celebrated directly or by implication in Yeats's *The Resur-
rection*, in Lawrence's *The Man Who Died*, and in many
other works of this century, becoming a recurrent symbol of
the sustained modern attempts to repaganize religious tradition. In his original mythical career, he suffers dismember-
ment, is made whole and reincarnated and then received
with love by the shades in Hades, and is reborn in the spring
as Dionysus, favored son of Zeus. Pound's Elysium is
Zagreus' also, a haven of pure, unabashed sexuality as in
Cantos 39 and 47. Elysium in the *Cantos*, however, is somewhat more cosmopolitan than Homer ever imagined. It has
room for gods, heroes, and nymphs from all cultures, for a

Renaissance figure like Sigismundo Malatesta whom Pound
presents as having fought a losing but unflagging battle
against the rise of the modern usury-dominated state, and
for thinkers like Confucius and the founding fathers of the
American Constitution. (See, for example, the great incantatory paean in Canto 106.)

The poet himself appears in the *Cantos* as a wandering
sensibility, seeking like Zagreus to reunite the essential self.
Even more, he is an Odysseus of the spirit, here as in
Mauberley seeking his true home and his true cultural mission and finding his bearing, amid the welter of historical
and ethical fragmentation, only by keeping forever in the
foreground of his consciousness the difference between the
life-bearing tradition and the death-dealing blight of Usura.
Canto 1, as we have noted, is a condensed translation of
The Book of the Dead: Book XI of the *Odyssey.* Here at the
start Pound identifies himself symbolically with Odysseus at
the point where the worlds of the living and the dead come
together (and by an easy enough association with Zagreus
also and with Dante on the verge of his explorations into the
horrors of his own day, projected in the *Inferno*).

Throughout the remaining cantos, the poet's moral sense,
as acute as and indeed of the same order as his other senses,
encompasses the whole of being, both experienced and imagined: life and death, mortals and immortals, heaven and
hell and earth, past and present. In Canto 16 we have a
concentrated Dantean view of the human condition, between Hell on the one hand and Purgatory and Paradise on
the other:

> And before hell mouth; dry plain
>   and two mountains;
> On the one mountain, a running form,
>   and another
> In the turn of the hill; in hard steel
> The road like a slow screw's thread,
> The angle almost imperceptible,
>   so that the circuit seemed hardly to rise.

Four figures of poets are discerned on this symbolic landscape; they are the Provençal troubadours Peire Cardinal
and Sordello of Mantua (Dante's admired guide for part of
the *Purgatorio*), Dante himself, and Blake. All are in their
several ways possessed by the inclusive meaning, awesome
in its implications for mankind, of the scene. But it is Blake,
the one modern among them and perhaps *the* poet before
Pound most deeply engaged by these awesome implications,
whose form we first see and who is described in most detail:

> And the running form, naked, Blake,
> Shouting, whirling his arms, the swift limbs,
> Howling against the evil,
> > his eyes rolling,
> Whirling like flaming cart-wheels,
> > and his head held ba.. .vard to gaze on the evil
> As he ran from it,
> > to be hid by ..e steel mountain,
> And when he sho. éd again from the north side;
> > his ey.s blazing toward hell mouth,
> His neck fc .vard . . . .

Despit. thi. moral purview, Pound does little talking
about "humanity" in general. The *Cantos* has been accused
of .arious aesthetic and intellectual derelictions but never of
"emotional slither." Its impersonality of method forestalls
such criticism. The intricately designed play of its voices and
the shifts of space, time, and personae (speaking-characters)
make it a dynamic presentation, closer to a motion picture
expertly and unsentimentally directed than to a simple cry
of the heart. By impersonality we do not mean absence of
feeling and viewpoint, but their objective presentation; modern literature has long been concerned to find ways to use
the raw materials of experience and imagination without
becoming merely confessional, whimsical, or arbitrary. Perhaps the best known statements of this aim are Yeats's poem
"Sailing to Byzantium" and Eliot's essay "Hamlet and His
Problems," which deals with the expression of emotion in

poetry and advances the famous definition of the "objective correlative" as a guide to such expression. But Pound is equally with the other two poets an exponent and exemplar of the deliberate transformation of personal motives into objectified projections that go beyond their psychological origins.

His method is clear enough, and can be understood and enjoyed by the reader long before the literal sense of many passages is grasped. Pound achieves dramatic impersonality as the playwright or the film director does, by letting his characters, his settings, his rhythms do the talking while, strictly speaking, he himself usually "stays out of it." He employs many spokesmen, as we have already suggested—Odysseus, Malatesta, Kung, Adams, and the others—to set up a composite, actively moving consciousness that emerges in varied forms and circumstances. Also, he sets *styles* against one another, each evocative of a whole complex of meanings: lyrical passages against satirical ones, rhetoric against anecdote, coarseness against elegance. Now he speaks in the idiom of Divus' fifteenth-century Latin translation from Homer, now in that of Ovid or Cavalcanti, and now in the drawl of a shrewd Yankee engineer or the bawdy brogue of an old Irish sailor. Again, the poem may shift into boisterous parody of Browning ("Oh to be in England now that Winston's out") or veer sharply into an echo of the speech in Eleanor of Aquitaine's court. The poem is *kept moving* by an alert, witty mind stocked with allusions and cross references, a mind so interesting that it holds attention even at its least appealing. As Yeats writes of the characters of Shakespearean tragedy, Pound never "breaks up his lines to weep." There are horror and terror, yes, but *sentimentality* is held to be a fraudulence of communication, the stylistic counterpart of usury. A striking instance of this viewpoint is Artemis' song against "pity" in Canto 30. Pity is a latter-day softmindedness, she cries, which "spareth so many an evil thing" that "all things are made foul in this season" of a liberal humanitarianism incapable of clear-cut moral distinctions or of root-solutions to the problems of suffering and evil:

> This is the reason, none may seek purity
> Having for foulnesse pity
> And things growne awry;
> No more do my shaftes fly
> To slay. Nothing is now clean slayne
> But rotteth away. . . .

Artemis' "compleynt" epitomizes one of Pound's major themes, but the poet does not state that theme directly. It is enough that the goddess is an embodiment of the ancient Grecian values, and the form of her song an embodiment of the medieval values, which we know he cherishes. She does his work for him, far more reverberatingly than his own haranguing could do it, and typifies the success of his presentational, or objective method.

3

The Mauberley *Sequence*

We have labeled the *Mauberley* poems and the *Cantos* "sequences," and it may help the general reader to be reminded of the implications of this label. Long poem-sequences are as familiar as, and much older than, the Elizabethan sonnet cycles, or as that cumbersomely unfolded series of allegorical narratives *The Faerie Queene*. In more recent times, to skip over innumerable other instances, we have Whitman's sequences, most notably his *Song of Myself;* and we must bear in mind Whitman's conception of the *whole* of his poetry as organically unified, the Self writ large: "Who touches these poems touches a man." A number of modern poets have turned to the sequence as a rough equivalent for the most ambitious traditional forms, and for the epic particularly. It may well have been Whitman who called this turn most decisively. At any rate, one has only to look at the song cycles of Yeats and the sequences of Eliot, Hart Crane, and a large number of other writers besides Pound to confirm this development.

The sequence is not a fixed form, and through this fact alone becomes very different from the classical elegy, ode, or epic. But we can say of it that in the work of the moderns from Whitman on it consists of a larger structure made up of more or less self-sufficient units, each contributing both conceptually and stylistically to the organic life of the whole. Some units, poems like the "Envoi" of *Mauberley* and Canto 13, are able to stand alone. Others are relatively more dependent on the rest, though they may be essential to the sequence. While the order of parts is as *necessary* as the poet can make it, the principle of the design may not make itself felt at first; on the other hand, though in theory *any* work of art will rearrange itself, so to speak, around whatever in it initially seizes upon our attention, the sequence (like the mural painting) seems to give us more freedom than other poetic forms to start from any point within it that we find convenient. With Pound especially the reader ought to take advantage of this characteristic. For instance, most of us would find the first part of *Mauberley* more quickly available than the second to our understanding, and within it we would find the second, fourth, and fifth poems, and probably the "Envoi," less demanding than the rest. Similarly 13 and 45 are certainly among the most readily intelligible of the *Cantos.* These six poems, therefore, are poems we can fruitfully read first in their respective sequences, together with whatever passages elsewhere along the line take our fancies.

Looking at the first section of *Mauberley* from this standpoint, we shall quickly light upon some salient characteristics. Poem II begins with a little battery of nervous rhymes contrasting the machine age's "aesthetic" with that of classicism:

> The age demanded an image
> Of its accelerated grimace,

> Something for the modern stage,
> Not, at any rate, an Attic grace . . . .

The nervous effect is created partly by the two feminine endings that follow upon one another, partly by the rhyming of stressed and unstressed syllable in alternate lines. The distorted picture called up by "accelerated grimace" shows the speaker's contempt for what the "age demanded." Pound underlines his contempt in the next two stanzas, coining a slogan for the age:

> Better mendacities
> Than the classics in paraphrase!

Our epoch, he says, "assuredly" prefers plaster to alabaster, a mass-produced art to "the 'sculpture' of rhyme."

Poem II is therefore an assault on the age. Moving on to Poem IV we find an even more typical piece of Poundian rhetorical verse. This poem must be read aloud if the full value of its cumulative compassion and anger is to be felt, but as a poem of profound disillusionment, one of the early literary reactions against the War and a forerunner of the many postwar novels expressing the same responses, what it has to say is perfectly clear. The young, whatever their motives for going to war, are the victims of "wastage as never before." Those who survive must return

> home to old lies and new infamy;
> usury age-old and age-thick
> and liars in public places. . . .

Though the mood here is a continuation of that in Poem II, bitterness and irony are progressively deepened right up to the final, climactic line: "laughter out of dead bellies." The next poem, the fifth, then makes another turn on the same subject: the War. The contrast between the young in all their quickness and fresh zest (described in two lines that have the restrained pathos of a Greek epitaph) and the civilization for which they have died is restated with superb poetic economy. Much of the work of contrast is done through an alliterative device, the linking of words beginning in *b*. First there is the word "best," to suggest the youthful dead themselves, and then in angry machine-gun bursts the words for a rotten society—"an old *b*itch gone in the teeth," "a *b*otched civilization"—and for its neglected heritage recalled only as a cynical pretext for inspiring the young in war: "two gross of *b*roken statues" and "a few thousand *b*attered *b*ooks."

"Envoi," which brings the 1919 section of *Mauberley* to a close, is not an assault on the times but an affirmation of artistic principle. Modeled on Edmund Waller's seventeenth-century poem "Go lovely rose," which was set to music by his contemporary Henry Lawes, it expresses the poet's desire to catch in an eternal moment one essence of both life and art in the image of a loved woman who sings out "that song of Lawes." There is an echo of Shakespeare when the speaker says he would bid "her graces" live

> As roses might, in magic amber laid,
> Red overwrought with orange and all made
> One substance and one colour
> Braving time.

And there is a carry-over from the aestheticism of the nineties in the thought with which the poem concludes, that immortality is to be gained only through artistic means which

> Might, in new ages, gain her worshippers,
> When our two dusts with Waller's shall be laid,
> Siftings on siftings in oblivion,
> Till change hath broken down
> All things save Beauty alone.

These four less difficult poems in the sequence throw enough light on the others to lead us directly to the perspective of the whole: We have moved into an age in which cheap standards of workmanship, anti-aestheticism, and the betrayal of beauty and tradition are the order of the day; but the poet does not accept this order. Rather, he lashes out against it, seeing in the destructiveness of the War its true, annihilating meaning. Through the perfection of his own craftsmanship in these poems, as well as through what he says, he affirms the superiority of his own vision.

Here, then, is the essence of the first section of *Mauberley*. But the sequence consists not merely of a few poems whose attitudes support and complement one another. It also takes the form of a kind of literary (but not literal) autobiography, in which the poet sizes up the state of the world of letters and his own place in it after three years of attempting to make himself and his viewpoint felt. In another sense, it takes the form of a voyage of literary exploration in contemporary England, with attention also to the condition of society at large and to the past circumstances out of which the present situation, at the end of the Great War, has developed. "The sequence," writes Pound, is "distinctly a farewell to London." It is also a crucial statement of the relation between poetry and Anglo-American culture as he sees it, and in the final balance it would seem to be a farewell to the illusion that there is any hope for poetry in that culture.

Going back to the beginning, we can see that although the protagonist of the sequence is the fictitious "Hugh Selwyn Mauberley" the first poem is titled "E. P. Ode pour l'Election de Son Sepulchre." Translated, this is "Ezra Pound, Ode on the Occasion of Choosing His Burial Place." (The self-ironic title is borrowed from a poem by Ronsard.) So Mauberley is Pound's conception of himself at one remove and in whatever dimensions these poems provide. Now who is Mauberley-Pound in this first poem? He is a man, the first two stanzas tell us, who has fought in vain against the drift of the times to "resuscitate the dead art/ Of poetry." But England has regarded him as hopelessly "out of key" with the age, especially as he has come from the United States, "a half savage country." Like Capaneus, who defied Zeus and was destroyed by lightning, he is a would-be hero victimized by his own hubris. The reference (to a figure in Aeschylus' play *The Seven Against Thebes*) leads to another classical allusion, this time to Book XII of the *Odyssey*, where the Sirens are shown singing their seductively compassionate song to Odysseus. The comparison between E. P. and Odysseus is developed over two stanzas, establishing an identification like that of the *Cantos*. He has lingered in the dangerous, choppy seas of the "rocks" of English culture; presumably he had cherished hopes that the superficial classical sophistication of the British literary and academic world was the real thing, and that he would find his true home, his Ithaca and Penelope, there. But his "true Penelope" was not the pretentious show-classicism of England but the dedicated, stylistically precise, unsqueamishly truthful art of Flaubert—the true classicism of the modern world. This point established, the last stanza returns to the mock-humble tone of the first with an echo from Villon's Grand Testament in which the poet talks of his own "passing away" in "the thirtieth year of his age" and with a final pompous comment on that event, in the voice of the chairman of some imaginary committee of literary stuffed shirts:

> . . . the case presents
> No adjunct to the Muses' diadem.

On the surface, this supremely ironic opening poem concedes defeat; actually, in various subtle ways, it asserts the continuing value of the poet's frustrated mission. Almost every line, by virtue of its very phrasing, proclaims the glory of "the tradition"; and the Homeric quotation near its center becomes, not only through what it says literally—"for we know all the things that are in Troy"—but also because of its cultural connotation *as* a Homeric quotation, a symbol in its own right. Even untranslated, it would serve as a symbol of the mystery behind the tradition, undefined though apparently related to the associations connected with Capaneus and Odysseus. Hence it should not surprise us that in the

next four poems the speaker breaks loose from the pretense
that he has been wrong to make his great effort. Rather, he
has been entranced by the Siren-song, and after locating
himself more accurately he can shift into the specifics of his
complaint against the world his art has been unable to affect.
Poem II is transitional, but Poem III is a *complete* list of
grievances, against the decadence of fashionable women's
clothing and their musical education as well as against the
loss of mystery in modern religion and the supposed empti-
ness of modern democracy. Lines 15–16 tell us once more
that nowadays we see The Beautiful "decreed in the market
place," and the poem ends with a mock-despairing cry to
Apollo which includes a quotation from Pindar translated
for us in the next line. (The "tin" of the last line is a flip
pun on the interrogative repeated three times in the Greek
quotation.)

   The reader will notice somewhere along the line that most
of the *Mauberley* poems are written in approximately the
same kind of stanza, a quatrain with alternating rhymes,
sometimes in the second and fourth lines only. There are
inconsistencies of line-length and rhyme-arrangement, but
the basic pattern holds even in Poem IV; "Envoi," it is true,
departs more than the others from it, but "Go lovely rose,"
on the form of which "Envoi" is a free variation, comes very
close to it. The "inconsistencies," of course, are deliberate
modulations to serve particular purposes, as when in Poem
IV the shortened lines and piled-up, almost doggerel rhymes
help to build up a quick emotional charge and an incantatory
rhythm, whereupon rhyme is dropped except for repetitions
and the stanzas are broken up into rhetorical units. In "E. P.
Ode," on the other hand, the lines are of uniform length and
the rhymes, though occasionally polylingual, are all exact.
The tone of elegant, subtle, literate intellectual control here
demands such exactness. "Envoi," in which the poet bursts
into a song whose mood counteracts the cutting, critical
drive of the sequence as a whole, is quite properly furthest
from the norm set up by the opening "Ode."

After the elegiac and savage climax of the fifth poem, the sequence shifts to some close-ups of the nineties and before. Here we see the beginnings of the modern predicament of the poet—the stuffiness of the late nineteenth century, the attack on the "fleshly school of poetry" by Robert Buchanan in 1871, the "stillbirth" twelve years before that of the English *Rubaiyat,* the abuse of Rossetti and Swinburne, and the relegation of the Muse to prostitute-status. The "Yeux Glauques" of the sixth poem refers to the "thin, clear gaze" of the Muse, here identified with the model for the Burne-Jones paintings alluded to in the third stanza, and also, by a shift of association, with the girl so compassionately presented in Rossetti's poem "Jenny." (Mrs. Rossetti was Burne-Jones's model.) In this period the dedicated artist not only saw his work disregarded, we are told; he also saw himself condemned as immoral. And so in the seventh poem, whose title alludes to the pathetic outcry in the *Purgatorio* of La Pia, we see, through the eyes of M. Verog (actually Victor Plarr, Dowson's biographer), how Dowson and Johnson met the hostile indifference to poetry in the nineties. In these poems Pound employs a number of allusions at first bewilderingly unfamiliar in order to recall the exact atmosphere of the times. But what stands out is the imagery connoting the defeat of art in England:

> Fœtid Buchanan lifted up his voice
> When that faun's head of hers
> Became a pastime for
> Painters and adulterers.

Even the incidental background descriptions carry this connotation of defeat:

> Among the pickled fœtuses and bottled bones . . . .

And here too we have echoes of the poet's ironic "confession" of error in Poem I:

> M. Verog, out of step with the decade,
> Detached from his contemporaries,
> Neglected by the young,
> Because of these reveries.

The portrait of "Brennbaum," a modern assimilated Jew who has all but forgotten his Hebraic heritage in his stiff, uncommunicatively British gentility, gives us yet another view of a society every phase of which reflects loss of meaning. Like Mr. Nixon, the literary businessman, and like the "conservatrix of Milésien" (in Poem XI) who lacks taste and the appreciation of tradition despite her pretensions, he symbolizes a condition which has made retreat or escape virtually a physical necessity for "the stylist" of Poem X. Nor can he look for literary patronage of the sort which came to an end in Dr. Johnson's day. As Poem XII shows, "The Lady Valentine" may use him to enhance her own social prestige, or to stimulate some incidental sexual excitement in her life, or, "in the case of revolution," as "a possible friend and comforter." But her "well-gowned approbation" will bring him no more real support than the world of professional letters will bring him now that, in Fleet Street,

> The sale of half-hose has
> Long since superseded the cultivation
> Of Pierian roses.

In the second portion of the *Mauberley* sequence (1920), all the themes we have noted are recapitulated, but with a difference. Whereas the speaker in the 1919 group had concentrated attention on specific points of attack in the "outside world" of society and of the cultural situation, bluntly challenging it with his own aesthetic values, his attention is now directed almost wholly inward. *Mauberley* (1919) is externalized, objective; *Mauberley* (1920) gives us the subjective dimension. Here the speaker is sure of his sensitivity but not of his strength as an artist; he discounts himself and withdraws, communicating his uncertainties and fear of failure. The epigraph, modified from Ovid's Latin, gives us an image of pure frustration: "mouths snapping at empty air." Poem I in this section, though it parallels its counterpart in the first movement, is developed in a series of elliptical sentences except for stanza two, in which the antecedent poem is quoted directly:

> "His true Penelope
> Was Flaubert,"
> And his tool
> The engraver's.

Whereas the first part of the sequence had spoken out for a virile, classically precise art in the great tradition, here the poet describes himself as having turned from delicate etching in the nineteenth century manner of Jaquemart to the skill of Roman and Renaissance medalists. That is, though he has turned from more effeminately ornamental minor artistry to a method informed by classical criteria, he is still working in a minor mode. He may approach the successes of a Pisanello, but he feels, or fears, he cannot approach the robust success of the great Greek masterpieces, cannot "forge Achaia" in the image of his Homeric visions. These thoughts come through as half-statements, expressing syntactically a dread of ultimate failure not unlike that of Browning's Andrea del Sarto or Eliot's Prufrock.

The speaker's fears are carried over subtly and somewhat ambiguously into Poem II. However, the French epigraph, actually Pound's own composition, extends the theme by introducing a new consideration: the relation between aesthetic sensitivity and the ability to know love in terms suggesting both delicate idealism and sensuality. The poem itself, introspective and elusive, employs a partly stream-of-consciousness method to describe and account for the failure of Mauberley's mission during the three lost years. He has been moving among phantasmagoria, among fantastic, illusory images of the night ("NUKTIS 'AGALMA"), finding his bearings and closing in on the "orchid" of his vision

of ideal beauty. But given his limited kind of talent, a talent
for making, in poetry, "curious heads in medallion," it is to
be doubted whether he can in any case realize his ideal. And
between the phantasmagoria on the one hand and this
newly recognized predicament on the other, he has somehow let go by the opportunity for love in its most full-blown
sense.

> He had passed, inconscient, full gaze,
> The wide-banded irides
> And botticellian sprays implied
> In their diastasis. . . .

Both a failure of sexual awareness (and perhaps perform-
ance) and a failure to see deeply enough into the orchid's
"botticellian" meaning (the reference is to the famous painting of the birth of Venus) to give it richly sensuous embodiment seem to be implied in this phrasing. The psychological
components of his failure to impress the public and of his
dismissal by his "self-styled 'his betters'" are a stale sensa-
tion of having missed out on the main chance and a distrust
of his own powers. In this poem Pound adds greatly to the
authority of his sequence, by giving Mauberley introspective
depth and body. It will be clear that the shadings and quali-
fications that so profoundly modify our understanding of the
speaker's whole nature here could not have been given before we had come to grips with the "outer" Mauberley-
Pound of the first part. We have seen him dressed for the
forum; now we see him naked and alone. "Envoi," which
presents the ideal he would live by, bridges the gap between
the two Mauberleys revealed with such moving and startling
faithfulness. But after the confession of Poem II and the
revisions of the Odysseus-image that follow in the next two
parts ("'The Age Demanded'" and Poem IV), "Medallion"
—the closing poem—throws a new light on the speaker's relation to the tradition as it was bravely proclaimed in
"Envoi."

But we are moving too quickly perhaps. To go back now

and follow through in order, " 'The Age Demanded' " takes its title, as the author's note reminds us, from the opening line in Poem II of *Mauberley* 1919. However, it focuses less on "the age" than on what the earlier piece, in its half-mimicry of Philistine criticism, calls "the obscure reveries of the inward gaze." Retreat to the world of these reveries is the poet's response to the age's demand for cheap, time-serving workmanship. As unfit for such drudgery as the doves that draw Aphrodite's chariot would be for a "chain bit," he has put on an "armour/Against utter consternation": the armour of imperviousness, impassive regression, and isolation. What Mauberley says of himself is of course true generally for the drift of modern poetry. Things, though, are not what they seem, for we know that the motives and meanings in which he deals, and in which the poets (like Pound) for whom he speaks deal, are anything but irrelevant. His fears are real but not finally decisive in his self-evaluation, a fact we need to remember as we see this psychological poetic *novella* in action and watch Mauberley's heroically active image of himself dwindle into that of the merest passive resistance and private self-delighting with "imaginary/Audition of the phantasmal sea-surge." Poem IV carries the dwindling of the image to its logical conclusion short of zero:

> "I was
> And I no more exist;
> Here drifted
> An hedonist."

Finally, "Medallion" portrays the singing lady of "Envoi" in a similarly shrunken imagery. The lovely singer at the piano is still conceived in terms of the service of Aphrodite. But the goddess herself (as Poem II showed) is not revealed in the full "diastasis" of Botticelli's conception; instead, she is seen through the medium of a lesser art, a Luini painting or the illustration in an archaeological study:

> As Anadyomene in the opening
> Pages of Reinach.

The Muse of "Yeux Glauques," though degraded and be-
wildered, had been more immediately womanly. Now, pro-
tected by glaze or a "suave bounding-line," she has a frozen
quality, is all unrealized potentiality in "metal, or intractable
amber."

But the potentiality remains; the strong and the weak
Mauberley are after all one and the same: a single *persona*
seen in opposing yet interactive lights.[13] Just as the *method*
of the Initial "Ode" counteracts its surface confession of
failure, so also does the extraordinary felicity of color, sound,
and nuance in the 1920 movement correct, if it does not
belie them entirely, the speaker's self-abnegations. Mauberley's confessions are really a charge of cultural failure from
the standpoint of the culture's own most cultivated sensibilities, and his psychological crisis becomes an expression of
despair for the future of social imagination and integrity. It
is not, finally, himself and his art that he denies but the
promise of his civilization. *Mauberley* (1920) is thus the
purest example we have of Pound's irony.

[13] Espey differs considerably from us on this point, although we
would certainly both agree that, as he says, "in the person of
Mauberley Pound was rejecting—though . . . this is altogether outside the limits of the poem . . .—a mask of what he feared to
become as an artist by remaining in England." (p. 83) The greatest
irony of *Mauberley* is the strength it gains from confessing vulner-
ability. The bawdy suggestiveness of Mauberley-Pound's language,
to which Espey calls our attention repeatedly, is one more instance
of his audacity and defiance in the midst of *apparent* confused
retreat.

4

The Cantos

Space forbids our going into the *Cantos* in even as much detail as we have into *Mauberley*. We have already, however, noted some of the leading ideas behind this more involved and ambitious work, and though we cannot here trace their handling throughout its winding, Gargantuan progress, a few suggestions concerning its character as a poetic sequence may be useful. First of all, we may take as our point of departure the fact that in motivation and outlook the *Cantos* are a vast proliferation from the same conceptions which underlie *Mauberley*. The difference lies partly in the multiplicity of "voices" and "cross-sections," partly in the vastly greater inclusiveness of historical and cultural scope, and partly in the unique formal quality of the longer sequence; it is by the very nature of its growth over the years a work-in-progress. Even when the author at last brings it to conclusion, reorganizing it, supplying the withheld Cantos 72 and 73, completing his revisions, and even giving his book a definitive title, it will remain such a work. Each group of cantos will be what it is now—a new *phase* of the poem, like each of the annual rings of a living tree. The poet has put his whole creative effort into a mobilization of all levels of his consciousness into the service of the *Cantos;* there has been a driving central continuity, and around it new clusters of knowledge and association linked with the others by interweavings, repetitions, and over-all perspective. Pound has staked most of his adult career as a poet on this most daring of poetic enterprises; literary history gives us few other examples of comparable commitment.

The *Cantos* has been called Pound's "intellectual diary since 1915," and so it is. But the materials of this diary have been so arranged as to subserve the aims of the poem itself. Passage by passage there is the fascination of listening in on a learned, passionate, now rowdy, now delicate intelligence, an intelligence peopled by the figures of living tradition but not so possessed by them that it cannot order their appearances and relationships. Beyond the fascination of the surface snatches of song, dialogue, and description, always stimulating and rhythmically suggestive though not always intelligible upon first reading, there is the essential overriding drive of the poem, and the large pattern of its overlapping layers of thought. The way in which the elements of this pattern swim into the reader's line of vision is well suggested by Hugh Kenner, one of Pound's most able and enthusiastic interpreters:

The word 'periplum,' which recurs continually throughout the *Pisan Cantos* [74–84], is glossed in Canto LIX:

> periplum, not as land looks on a map
> but as sea bord seen by men sailing.

Victor Brerard discovered that the geography of the *Odyssey*, grotesque when referred to a map, was minutely accurate according to the Phoenician voyagers' *periploi*. The image of successive discoveries breaking upon the consciousness of the voyager is one of Pound's central themes. . . . The voyage of Odysseus to hell is the matter of Canto I. The first half of Canto XL is a periplum through the financial press; 'out of which things seeking an exit,' we take up in the second half of the Canto the narrative of the Carthagenian Hanno's voyage of discovery. Atlantic flights in the same way raise the world of epileptic maggots in Canto XXVIII into a sphere of swift firm-hearted discovery. . . . The periplum, the voyage of discovery among facts, . . . is everywhere contrasted with the conventions and artificialities of the bird's eye view afforded by the map. . . .[14]

Thus, the successive cantos and layers of cantos must be viewed not so much schematically as experientially. Here we see how the early Pound's developing idealization of the concrete image, the precise phrase, the organically accurate rhythm are now brought to bear on this vast later task. The many voices, varied scenes and *personae*, and echoes of other languages and literatures than English reflect this emphasis on experience itself: something mysterious, untranslatable, the embodied meaning of life which we generalize only at peril of losing touch with it. So also with Pound's emphatic use of Chinese ideograms, whose picture-origins still are visible enough, he believes, so that to "read" them is to think in images rather than in abstractions. His use of them is accounted for by the same desire to present "successive discoveries breaking upon the consciousness of the voyager." The first effect of all these successive, varied breakings is not intended to be total intellectual understanding, any more than in real experience we "understand" situations upon first coming into them. But by and by the pattern shapes up

[14] Hugh Kenner, *The Poetry of Ezra Pound* (Norfolk, Conn.: New Directions, 1951), pp. 102–103. Kenner's use of Roman numerals follows Pound, but the latest groups of cantos (*Rock-Drill* and *Thrones*), published after Kenner's book, change to Arabic numerals. For consistency's sake we have followed the latter usage throughout.

and the relationships clarify themselves, though always there
remains an unresolved residue of potentiality for change, intractable and baffling.

Pound's "voyager," upon whose consciousness the discoveries break, is, we have several times observed, a composite figure derived first of all from the poet-speaker's
identification with Odysseus. A hero of myth and epic, he is
yet very much of this world. He is both the result of creative
imagination and its embodiment. He explores the worlds of
the living, of the dead, and of the mythic beings of Hades
and Paradise. Lover of mortal women as of female deities,
he is like Zagreus a symbol of the life-bringing male force
whose mission does not end even with his return to his
homeland. Gradually he becomes all poets and all heroes
who have somehow vigorously impregnated the culture. He
undergoes (as do the female partners of his procreation and
the *personae* and locales in time and space of the whole sequence) many metamorphoses. Hence the importance of the
Ovidian metamorphosis involving the god Dionysus, the sea
(the female element and symbol of change), and the inter-
mingling of contemporary colloquial idiom and the high
style of ancient poetry in Canto 2. The first canto had ended
with a burst of praise for Aphrodite, goddess of love and
beauty, and in language suggesting the multiple allusiveness
of the sequence: to the Latin and Renaissance traditions, as
well as the Grecian-Homeric, and to the cross-cultural implications suggested by the phrase "golden bough." The second
canto takes us swiftly backward in the poetic tradition,
through Browning, then Sordello and the other troubadours,
and then to the classical poets and the Chinese tradition.
All poets are one, as Helen and Eleanor of Aquitaine and
Tyro (beloved of Poseidon) and all femininity are one and
all heroes are one.

In the first two cantos, then, the "periplum" of the sequence emerges into view. Three main value-referents are
established: a sexually and aesthetically creative world-view,
in which artistic and mythical tradition provides the main

axes; the worship of Bacchus-Dionysus-Zagreus as the best symbol of creativity in action; and the multiple hero—poet, voyager, prophet, observer, thinker. The next four cantos expand the range of allusiveness, introducing for instance the figure of the Cid, a chivalric hero, to add his dimension to the voyager-protagonist's consciousness. Also, various tragic tales are brought to mind, extending the initial horror of Odysseus' vision of the dead and thus contributing to the larger scheme of the poet in the modern wasteland. In absolute contrast, pagan beatitudes are clearly projected in Canto 2 in the pictures of Poseidon and Tyro:

> Twisted arms of the sea-god,
> Lithe sinews of water, gripping her, cross-hold,
> And the blue-gray glass of the wave tents them . . . .

and, at the scene's close, in the phallic "tower like a one-eyed great goose" craning up above the olive grove while the fauns are heard "chiding Proteus" and the frogs "singing against the fauns." This pagan ideal comes in again and again, sharp and stabbing against bleak backgrounds like the "petals on the wet, black bough" of the "Metro" poem. Thus, in Canto 3:

> Gods float in the azure air,
> Bright gods and Tuscan, back before dew was shed.

In Canto 4:

> Choros nympharum, goat-foot, with the pale foot alternate;
> Crescent of blue-shot waters, green-gold in the shallows,
> A black cock crows in the sea-foam . . . .

In 4 and 5 both there are deliberate echoes of such poets as have a kindred vision (Catullus, Sappho, and others), set against the notes of evil and damnation. The lines from Sordello in 6 serve the same purpose:

"Winter and Summer I sing of her grace,
As the rose is fair, so fair is her face,
Both Summer and Winter I sing of her,
The snow makyth me to remember her."

The Lady of the troubadours, whose "grace" is a secularized transposition from that of Deity, is another manifestation of "the body of nymphs, of nymphs, and Diana" which Actaeon saw, as well as of what Catullus meant: " 'Nuces!' praise, and Hymenaeus 'brings the girl to her man. . . .' "

After these archetypal and literary points of reference have been established, Cantos 8–19 move swiftly into a close-up of the origins of the modern world in the Renaissance, and of the victory of the anticreative over the active, humanistic values represented by Sigismundo Malatesta and a few others. (Canto 7 is transitional; in any case we can note only the larger groupings here.) The relation between the "Renaissance Cantos" (8–11) and the "Hell Cantos" (14–16), with their scatological picturings of the contemporary Inferno, is organic: the beginning and the end of the same process of social corruption. The beautiful dialogue on order in 13 provides a calm, contrasting center for this portion of the sequence, and is supported by the paradisic glow and serenity of Elysium, revealed in 16 and 17. The earlier cantos had given momentary attention to Oriental poetry and myth and, as we have seen, Elysian glimpses also. Now these motifs are expanded and related to a new context, bringing the sequence into revised focus but carrying all its earlier associations along. This leaping, reshuffling, and reordering is the organizational principle behind the growth, the "annual rings," of the *Cantos*.

The next ten cantos interweave the motifs of these first two groups and prepare us for the next leap (in Cantos 30–41) of perspective. There are various preparations for this leap, even as early as Canto 20, in which there is a moment of comment from the "outside" as if to take stock before hurtling onward. From their remote "shelf," "aerial, cut in the aether," the disdainful lotus-eaters question all purposeful effort:

> "What gain with Odysseus,
> "They that died in the whirlpool
> "And after many vain labours,
> "Living by stolen meat, chained to the rowingbench,
> "That he should have a great fame
>   "And lie by night with the goddess? . . ."

Is the question wisdom or cynicism? No matter. The poem, given the human condition and the epic tasks that grow out of it, is held in check but an instant before again plunging ahead. The *Cantos* accepts the moral meaning and the moral responsibility of human consciousness. The heroic ideal remains, as on the other hand the evil of our days remains even after the goddess' song against pity is heard at the beginning of 30.

The new group (30–41) is, like the later Adams cantos (62–71), in the main a vigorous attempt to present the fundamental social and economic principles of the Founding Fathers as identical with Pound's own. Adams and Jefferson are his particular heroes, and there is an effort to show that Mussolini's program is intended to carry these basic principles, imbedded in the Constitution but perverted by banking interests, into action. Pound works letters and other documents, as well as conversations real and imagined, into his blocks of verse, usually fragmentarily, and gives modern close-ups of business manipulations. The method has the effect of a powerful exposé, particularly of the glimpsed operations of munitions-profiteers. The cantos of the early 1930's have, indeed, a direct connection with the interest in social and historical documentation and rhetoric that marks much other work of the same period, and at the end of Canto 41 (in which Mussolini is seen) we should not be surprised to find an oratorical climax similar in effect to that of Poem IV in *Mauberley* (1919). As in the earlier groups, however, we are again given contrasting centers of value, especially in Canto 36 (which renders Cavalcanti's *A lady asks me*) and in Canto 39, whose sexually charged interpretation of the spell cast over Odysseus and his men on Circe's isle is one of Pound's purest successes.

The Chinese cantos (53–61) and the Pisan group (74–84) are the two most important remaining unified clusters within the larger scheme. Again, the practical idealism of Confucianism, like that of Jefferson and Adams, becomes an analogue for Pound's own ideas of order and of secular aestheticism. Canto 13 was a clear precursor, setting the poetic stage for this later extension. "Order" and "brotherly deference" are key words in Confucius' teachings; both princes and ordinary men must have order *within* them, each in his own way, if dominion and family alike are to thrive. These thoughts are not clichés as Pound presents them. We hear a colloquy that has passion, humor, and depth, and what our society would certainly consider unorthodoxy. Kung "said nothing of the 'life after death,'" he considered loyalty to family and friends a prior claim to that of the law, he showed no respect for the aged when they were ignorant through their own fault, and he advocated a return to the times "when the historians left blanks in their writings,/I mean for things they didn't know." The Chinese cantos view Chinese history in the light of these principles of ordered intelligence in action, with the ideogram *ching ming* (name things accurately) at the heart of the identity between Confucian and Poundian attitudes. "The great virtue of the Chinese language," writes Hugh Gordon Porteus, "inheres in its written characters, which so often contrive to suggest by their graphic gestures (as English does by its phonetic gestures) the very essence of what is to be conveyed." [15] The development of Pound's interest in Chinese poetry and thought, as well as his varied translations from the Chinese, is in itself an important subject. This interest, like every other to which he has seriously turned his

[15] "Ezra Pound and the Chinese Character: A Radical Examination," in *Ezra Pound*, p. 215.

attention, he has brought directly to bear on his own poetic practice and on his highly activistic thinking in general.

With the *Pisan Cantos* and *Rock-Drill* [16] we are brought, first, into the immediately contemporary world of the poet himself, in Fascist Italy toward the close of World War II, in a concentration camp at Pisa, during the last days of Mussolini; and second, into a great, summarizing recapitulation of root-attitudes developed in all the preceding cantos: in particular the view of the banking system as a scavenger and breeder of corruption, and of ancient Chinese history as an illuminating, often wholesomely contrasting analogue to that of the post-medieval West. Even more than before, we see now how the *Cantos* descend, with some bastardies along the line, from the Enlightenment. They conceive of a world creatively ordered to serve human needs, a largely rationalist conception. Hence the stress on the sanity of Chinese thought, the immediacy of the Chinese ideogram, and the hardheaded realism of a certain strain of economic theory. The *Pisan Cantos* show Pound's vivid responsiveness as he approached and passed his sixtieth birthday: his aliveness to people, his Rabelaisian humor, his compassion. The Lotus-Eaters of Canto 20, aloof and disdainful, have missed out on the main chances. Canto 81 contains the famous "Pull down thy vanity" passage in which the poet, though rebuking his own egotism, yet staunchly insists on the meaningfulness of his accomplishment and ideals. As the sequence approaches conclusion, the fragments are shored together for the moral summing-up. In the *Rock-Drill* section, Cantos 85–95, the stocktaking continues and we are promised, particularly in Canto 90, an even fuller revelation than has yet been vouchsafed us of the Earthly Paradise.

Cantos 96–109 [17] begin to carry out this promise, though after so many complexities, overlappings, and interlocking

[16] Section: *Rock-Drill: 85–95 de los cantares* (New York: New Directions, 1956). This was the first group of cantos to be published separately since the *Cantos* appeared in 1948.

[17] *Thrones: 96–109 de los cantares* (New York: New Directions, 1959).

voices it must be nearly impossible to bring the work to an end. It is essentially a self-renewing process rather than a classical structure, and there is no limit to the aspects of history and thought the poet has wished to bring to bear on the poem. Canto 96, for instance, touches on certain developments after the fall of Rome, especially two decrees in the Eastern Empire by Justinian and Leo VI concerning standards of trade, workmanship, and coinage. The special emphasis in this canto on Byzantine civilization is particularly appropriate because of Byzantium's historical and geographical uniting of East and West as well as its mystical associations pointing to a new and dramatic paradisic vision. Although the memory of earlier glimpses of "paradise" and the recapitulative, self-interrupting method militate against an effect of a revelation overwhelmingly new, the pacing of the whole sequence has made this difficulty at the end inevitable. Pound's conclusion must be introduced as emergent from the midst of things, still struggling from all in life and consciousness that makes for disorder.

5

Envoy

Pound's career has been a long one and a various one. We have attempted a brief review of his early development, of his basic attitudes, and of his two major sequences. Clearly, a very great deal still remains to be said, not only about the poetry we have been able to touch on but also about work not even mentioned thus far, such as *Cathay* and *Homage to Sextus Propertius*. The interested reader will find detailed exposition in a number of valuable studies, among them Hugh Kenner's *The Poetry of Ezra Pound*, John Espey's *Ezra Pound's* Mauberley, Harold H. Watts's *Ezra Pound and the Cantos*, and Clark Emery's *Ideas into Action*. Peter Russell's collection *Ezra Pound* contains useful essays by numerous authors on important aspects of Pound's writing, and elsewhere there are valuable scattered pieces and passages by Louis Zukofsky, T. S. Eliot, William

Butler Yeats, F. R. Leavis, Horace Gregory, R. P. Blackmur, and others. Two mimeographed periodicals, *The Analyst* (Northwestern University) and *The Pound Newsletter* (University of California), and Edwards and Vasse's *Annotated Index to the Cantos of Ezra Pound* provide indispensable scholarly aids. But the best commentary on Pound is his own prose (including his letters) and verse. These remain the expression of one of our truly creative spirits, a poet who, not only a true "maker" in his own right, has been the begetter of creativity in countless others.

Selected Bibliography

WORKS

POETRY

The Cantos of Ezra Pound (N.Y.: New Directions, 1948).
Cantos 1–71 and 74–84.

Personae: The Collected Poems of Ezra Pound (N.Y.: Horace
Liveright, 1926; reprinted with additional poems, N.Y.:
New Directions, 1949).

Section: Rock-Drill: 85–95 de los cantares (N.Y.: New Directions, 1956). Cantos 85–95.

The Selected Poems of Ezra Pound (N.Y.: New Directions,
1949).

Thrones: 96–109 de los cantares (N.Y.: New Directions, 1959).
Cantos 96–109.

The Translations of Ezra Pound (N.Y.: New Directions, n. d.
[1954]).

54

PROSE

ABC of Reading (London: G. Routledge and Sons, 1934; New Haven: Yale University Press, 1934; Norfolk, Conn.: New Directions, 1951).

Jefferson and/or Mussolini (London: S. Nott, 1935; N.Y.: Liveright, 1935).

The Letters of Ezra Pound: 1907–1941, ed. D. D. Paige (N.Y.: Harcourt, Brace, 1950).

Literary Essays, ed. T. S. Eliot (Norfolk, Conn.: New Directions, 1954).

Money Pamphlets by £, 6 v. (London: Peter Russell, 1950–1952).

The Unwobbling Pivot and the Great Digest (N.Y.: New Directions, 1947).

COMMENTARY

The Analyst, ed. Robert Mayo. Evanston: Northwestern University, Department of English, 1953–   . This mimeographed publication, appearing "at intervals," has been in the main devoted to annotation of the *Cantos,* prepared by various hands.

Blackmur, R. P. *Language as Gesture* (N.Y.: Harcourt, Brace, 1952).

Edwards, John H. *A Preliminary Checklist of the Writings of Ezra Pound* (New Haven: Kirgo-Books, 1953).

Edwards, John H. and William W. Vasse. *Annotated Index to the Cantos of Ezra Pound* (Berkeley and Los Angeles: University of California Press, 1957).

Eliot, T. S. *Ezra Pound, His Metric and Poetry* (N.Y.: A. A. Knopf, 1917).

Emery, Clark. *Ideas into Action: A Study of Pound's Cantos* (Coral Gables, Fla.: University of Miami Press, 1958).

Espey, John. *Ezra Pound's Mauberley* (Berkeley and Los Angeles: University of California Press, 1955).

Gregory, Horace, and Zaturenska, Marya. *A History of American Poetry 1900–1940* (N.Y.: Harcourt, Brace, 1946).

Kenner, Hugh. *The Poetry of Ezra Pound* (Norfolk, Conn.: New Directions, 1951; London: Faber and Faber, 1951).

Leavis, F. R. *New Bearings in English Verse* (London: Chatto and Windus, 1932).

O'Connor, William Van and Edward Stone. *A Casebook on Ezra Pound* (N.Y.: Thomas Y. Crowell, 1959).

The Pound Newsletter, ed. John H. Edwards (Berkeley: University of California, 1954–1956). Ten issues of this mimeographed publication appeared, providing invaluable information and comment on Pound bibliography, various aspects of Pound's thought and career, aspects of the *Cantos,* and so on. See Number 10 (April, 1956) for Index to series.

Russell, Peter, ed. *Ezra Pound* (London: Peter Nevill, 1950; Norfolk, Conn.: New Directions, 1950). Published also by New Directions as *An Examination of Ezra Pound.*

Watts, Harold H. *Ezra Pound and the Cantos* (Chicago: H. Regnery, 1952).

Williams, William Carlos. *The Autobiography of William Carlos Williams* (N.Y.: Random House, 1951).

Yeats, William Butler. *A Packet for Ezra Pound* (Dublin: The Cuala Press, 1929). Reprinted in *A Vision* (London: Macmillan, 1937; N.Y.: Macmillan, 1938, 1956).

Zukofsky, Louis. "The Cantos of Ezra Pound," *The Criterion,* X (April, 1931), pp. 424–440.

A Primer of Ezra Pound

By M. L. Rosenthal:

A Primer of Ezra Pound

Exploring Poetry (WITH A. J. M. SMITH)